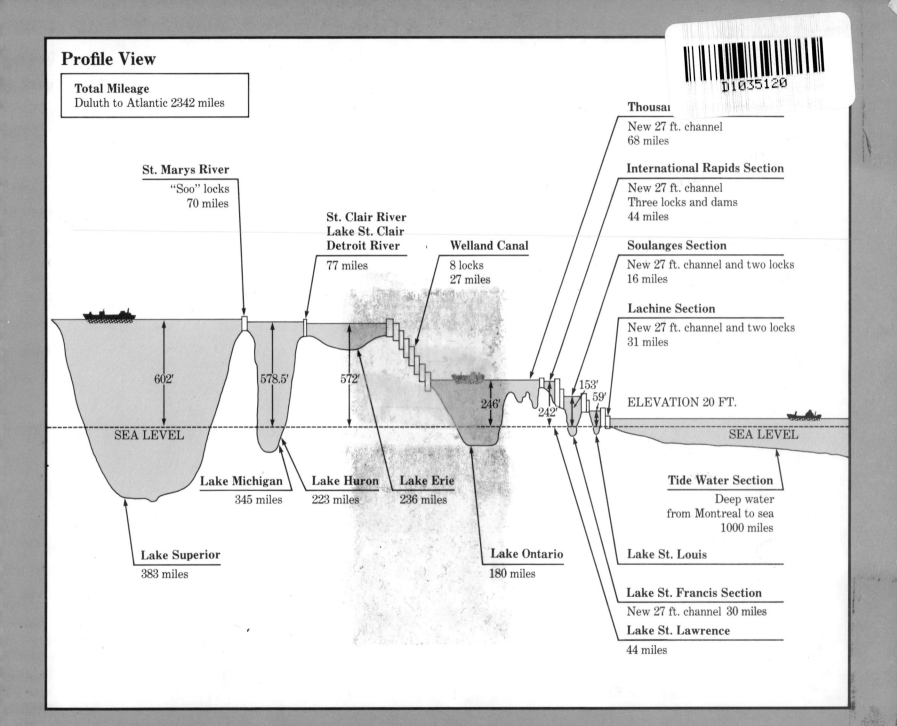

Profile View

Total Mileage
Duluth to Atlantic 2342 miles

St. Marys River
"Soo" locks
70 miles

St. Clair River
Lake St. Clair
Detroit River
77 miles

Welland Canal
8 locks
27 miles

Thousa[...]
New 27 ft. channel
68 miles

International Rapids Section
New 27 ft. channel
Three locks and dams
44 miles

Soulanges Section
New 27 ft. channel and two locks
16 miles

Lachine Section
New 27 ft. channel and two locks
31 miles

ELEVATION 20 FT.

602'

578.5'

572'

246'

242'

153'

59'

SEA LEVEL

SEA LEVEL

Lake Michigan
345 miles

Lake Huron
223 miles

Lake Erie
236 miles

Lake Ontario
180 miles

Lake Superior
383 miles

Tide Water Section
Deep water
from Montreal to sea
1000 miles

Lake St. Louis

Lake St. Francis Section
New 27 ft. channel 30 miles

Lake St. Lawrence
44 miles

The

Seaway

In commemoration of

the 20th anniversary of the Seaway
   and

the 150th anniversary of the
first Welland Canal

   1829   1959   1979

Robert F. Legget, O.C.

With a Foreword by
the Honourable Lionel Chevrier, P.C., C.C., Q.C.

Clarke, Irwin & Co. Ltd., Toronto/Vancouver

Canadian Cataloguing in Publication Data

Legget, Robert F., 1904-
  The Seaway

ISBN 0-7720-1270-9

1. St. Lawrence Seaway — History. 1. Title.

FC2763.2.L43   386'.5   C79-094305-0
HE635.Z7S25

© Minister of Supply and Services Canada 1979

Govt. catalogue no. TS3-8/1979

ISBN 0-7720-1270-9

1 2 3 4 5 83 82 81 80 79

Printed in Canada

Published by Clarke Irwin and Company Limited in co-operation with the St. Lawrence Seaway Authority and the Canadian Government Publishing Centre.

Contents

The St. Lawrence Seaway Authority

Presidents

1954-1957	*The Hon. Lionel Chevrier*
1957-1958	*Charles Gavsie*
1958-1960	*B.J. Roberts*
1960-1965	*R.J. Rankin*
1965-1973	*Pierre Camu*
1973-	*Paul D. Normandeau*

Members

1954-1957	*Charles Gavsie*
1954-1959	*C.W. West*
1957-1960	*J.-C. Lessard*
1960-1965	*Pierre Camu*
1963-1973	*P.E.R. Malcolm*
1965-1971	*D.E. Taylor*
1973-1977	*T.J. Quigg*
1973-	*H.G. Barrett*
1977-	*Marc Masson Bienvenu*

Foreword

As one who was born and brought up on the banks of the St. Lawrence River and later spent three strenuous and stimulating years as President of the St. Lawrence Seaway Authority during the period of construction of the deep waterway, I have derived a great deal of pleasure from reading Robert Legget's profusely illustrated account of the evolution of the St. Lawrence Seaway.

The story of how the natural waterway created by the St. Lawrence River and the Great Lakes was transformed by generations of human effort into a navigable 3750-kilometre transportation artery linking the Atlantic Ocean with the vast heartland of North America is one that has fascinated politicians, historians and businessmen for many years. To tame the rapids of the St. Lawrence and Niagara rivers, and to raise ships from tidewater to Lake Superior, some 180 metres above sea level, was an enormous task and it took more than 250 years before the present system evolved. It began in the 18th century with knee-deep canals equipped with primitive wooden locks that allowed fur traders' bateaux to circumvent the impassable St. Lawrence rapids and culminated in 1959 with the opening of the Seaway, a giant staircase of 23 huge concrete locks and 16 separate lifts, ranging from one metre at Iroquois on the St. Lawrence to the nearly 40-metre climb up the Niagara escarpment through the twinned flight locks of the Welland Canal at St. Catharines.

The Seaway is truly an engineering marvel but I know from personal experience that it took more than engineers to make it a reality. Never before had two sovereign nations such as the United States and Canada co-operated to produce works, both navigation and power, of such size. Few projects had been so bitterly opposed or inspired so many studies, arguments, legal battles, treaties and inter-governmental memoranda. Few projects were so desperately needed while being delayed for so long. The Seaway story is a chronicle of men fighting for self-interest against nations fighting for national interest.

Canadians can look back with pride on the drive and determination of those who kept the Seaway dream alive and pushed it through to completion. And now we celebrate twenty years of successful operation of the St. Lawrence-Great Lakes system and, coincidentally, the 150th anniversary of an integral part of that system, the Welland Canal. On such an occasion it is eminently fitting that the Seaway story should be told again — and Robert Legget has told it well.

THE SEAWAY is the name given to the modern development of the River St. Lawrence which permits large ocean-going vessels to sail into the heartland of North America. The largest lake freighters now bring their loads of grain down the Seaway to ocean ports, and sail back from salt water with iron ore from Labrador for steel mills around the Great Lakes. This magnificent inland waterway had been a dream since the very earliest days of commercial transport on the Lakes. As long ago as 1801, Sir Alexander Mackenzie, already famous as the explorer of the river which now bears his name and as the first man to reach the Pacific Ocean "overland from Montreal", proposed something very like the Seaway of today. In a memorandum to Lord Hobart, then British Secretary for War and the Colonies, he advocated a canal down the St. Lawrence between Lake Ontario and Montreal which "would render fruitless" the Erie Canal in the United States of America, then being discussed. Fifty years later, the first small seaway was ready for use, but it was to take another century before Mackenzie's dream was truly fulfilled.

Although all the earlier and smaller St. Lawrence canals had been built in and by Canada, the Seaway and the associated power development were constructed by Canada and the United States of America working harmoniously together. This vast undertaking was probably the largest engineering work yet carried out jointly by two neighbouring nations, continuing the long record of international co-operation in the use of the great river. Ships of both countries used the first Welland Canal, opened in 1829, which had been built by Canadians as were all other canals on the St. Lawrence-Great Lakes system. The modern Seaway was opened in 1959. The year 1979 therefore marks a joint anniversary of 150 years of service by successive Welland Canals, and the first twenty years of service of the Seaway. This volume has been produced by the St. Lawrence Seaway Authority to mark this significant occasion. It is a tribute also to the work of all those who have laboured to improve navigation on the St. Lawrence, down through three centuries, work to which this account is but an introduction.

* * *

Sieur Samuel de Champlain de Brouage — the great and good man known to all Canadians as the founder of their country — was the first white man to see the Great Lakes and to record his pioneer journey up from the sea. He was probably preceded by two young assistants whom he sent up the Ottawa with his Indian friends but they left no record of their travels. Champlain himself, however, recorded faithfully in his journals his journey in 1613 from Quebec to Montreal and then up the Ottawa River as far as Pembroke. He made his second western journey in 1615 when he traversed the entire Ottawa Waterway from Montreal, up the Ottawa and Mattawa Rivers, through Lake Nipissing and down the French River to Georgian Bay on Lake Huron. He later crossed the eastern end of Lake Ontario on 5 September 1615 (by "island-hopping" from Amherst Island) in company with his Indian hosts, for their attack upon the Iroquois and so must have heard about the upper St. Lawrence. It is significant, however, that he returned to Quebec, in 1616, by way of the Ottawa River, this being the then well recognized Indian route between the Great Lakes, Quebec and Tadoussac, and so to the Gulf of St. Lawrence and the Atlantic Ocean.

Champlain's example inspired others to follow his route to the Lakes — heroic Jesuit priests, and intrepid young *coureurs des bois* combining fur-trading, both legal and illegal, with exploration. All had to get past the Lachine rapids before entering Lake St. Louis, at the west end of which the Ottawa joins the St. Lawrence. A portage road, between present-day Montreal and Lachine, was the first "improvement" to this major water route of North America. For much of its length, this road ran close to the small Rivière St. Pierre, an extension of which would have enabled travellers to float their canoes along most of the portage. The Superior of the Sulpician Order in Montreal, Dollier de Casson, had the idea of a small "canal" which would achieve this purpose and first pro-

posed this in 1680. It was not until 1700 that a contract was awarded to Gedeon de Catalogne, but he went bankrupt when only 800 yards of the small ditch remained to be excavated. Available funds ran out and since the authorities in France were not too interested in spending money in the forests of Canada, then or later, the work lapsed and was never completed. The little ditch, however, remains significant as the beginning of improvements to the St. Lawrence, now almost three hundred years ago.

The name Lachine — originally La Chine — is a continuing reminder of the high hopes of the early adventurers that up the Great River (the

10 *Canoes in rapids on the St. Lawrence in 1760, by T. Davies.*

Ottawa) they would find a way to the East and all the wealth of China. One of them even included a damask robe in his meagre baggage, to wear on his arrival. Although the route to China proved to be just a dream, trade with the Indians for the furs they trapped — especially beaver — quickly grew into a formidable enterprise. Throughout the eighteenth century, the Ottawa River continued to be the prime route not only of the fur-traders but also of the explorers of all the Great Lakes, the mid-West, and eventually the North and the Pacific Coast.

This is at first surprising since the St. Lawrence route to Lake Ontario was discovered in 1669 by one of the early travellers on the Ottawa. Niagara Falls, leading to Lake Erie, was first seen by a white man in 1678. Both routes to the West involved journeying past turbulent rapids and falls, large and small; the Ottawa route was shorter but along the St. Lawrence it was up all the way, whereas those who used the Ottawa Waterway had to mount to the summit level of Trout Lake (near North Bay) and then descend along the French River into Georgian Bay. Despite this, the Ottawa River continued to be the main route to the West, precursor of the first Seaway, until the early years of the nineteenth century. Comte de Frontenac,

Rapids on the St. Lawrence near Cedars, with Indian travellers; 1838, by Coke Smyth.

another outstanding figure in early Canadian history, was a pioneer in the development of the way to the West by way of the St. Lawrence. He established in 1675 the Fort which bore his name, and which was the origin of the modern city of Kingston. Thereafter, some of the canoe traffic to the Great Lakes used the St. Lawrence but the formidable crossing of the Niagara Peninsula, into Lake Erie, constituted a real obstacle.

The First Canals

IT WAS not until General Sir Frederick Haldimand became Governor-in-Chief of Canada in 1778 that attention was given to the possibility of improving the St. Lawrence route. The new Governor was anxious to do everything possible to prevent valuable traffic in furs being diverted to trading posts in the United States. Improving the St. Lawrence route was one clearly desirable step and so the Governor had a survey made, by officers of the Corps of Royal Engineers of the

British Army, of the possibility of easing the passage through the rapids of the Soulanges section of the River, between Lake St. Louis and Lake St. Francis. Captain Twiss, R.E., duly reported; construction was authorized in 1779 and by 1781 four small canals had been completed, with the aid of Cornish miners brought from England to assist with rock excavation. The canals were located at Faucille Rapids (one lock), Trou du Moulin (one lock), Split Rock (no locks) and Coteau du Lac (three locks), and were quite small, being only six to seven feet wide with two feet six inches of water over the lock sills. They did facilitate the passage of bateaux past the rapids, however, and despite difficulties caused by ice damage in winter, they served until the early eighteen hundreds. They were then studied by Colonel Gother Mann, R.E., and subsequently rebuilt by the Royal Engineers with enlarged locks capable of handling Durham boats which could carry loads up to 35 tons. The rebuilt "Engineer Canals" served well until they were replaced in 1845. Small though they were, they occupy an important place in the long story which culminates in the Seaway of today.

It is surprising, at first sight, that Governor Haldimand should have concentrated his attention upon circumventing the rapids of the Soulanges

One of the early "Engineer" locks at Cascades, as seen in 1820 by William Roebuck.

13

An early view of masonry construction on the Lachine Canal.

section of the St. Lawrence while the Lachine Rapids constituted such a major obstacle to river traffic so close to Montreal. Study of the records left by some of the early travellers to the West provides a clue to the Governor's priorities. There existed a reasonable portage road from Montreal to Lachine over which the limited loads conveyed by bateaux and Durham boats could readily be transported on simple carts. Lachine gradually came to be adopted as the main "marine terminal" (to use a modern expression for a very simple facility) for the journeys to and from the Great Lakes. The portage road was later extended to Ste-Anne de Bellevue and regularly used in the early nineteenth century by passengers embarking on the journey up the Ottawa River. But change was in the air, dramatically indicated by the launching in 1809 by John Molson of Montreal of the first steamboat on the St. Lawrence.

The *Accommodation* was little more than a barge with a steam engine (made by Boulton and Watt) mounted upon its deck, but far-sighted merchants of Montreal realized its significance. Its success in providing a regular service between Montreal and Quebec gave new impetus to the demands for a canal linking Montreal and Lachine. Defence requirements led a new Governor to propose to the Legislature of Lower Canada in 1815 the start of a real Lachine Canal, but his proposal was not accepted and even the efforts of a joint stock company, founded by Montreal merchants in 1819, failed to get work started. In 1821, the provincial government appointed Commissioners to undertake the building of the canal, the Imperial (British) Government making a grant of £10,000 on condition that military supplies be conveyed free of charge through the Canal when completed. The Commissioners directed the work to such good effect that this first Lachine Canal was officially opened in 1825. It was Canada's first "modern"

Montreal. 1826

Entrance lock to the first Lachine Canal; from a watercolour of 1826.

canal, having a river or guard lock and six lifting locks, each 100 feet long and 20 feet wide with five feet of water over the lock sills, dimensions which must have seemed large at the time, but which were very soon found to be inadequate.

An early view on the Lachine Canal.

16

The War of 1812 and Canals

THE DEFENCE requirements arose from the War of 1812, the last conflict between British North America (the Canada of today) and the United States of America. Often referred to as "Mr. Madison's war", it should never have started and probably would not have commenced if a trans-Atlantic cable had then been in existence. It was terminated by the Treaty of Ghent, signed on Christmas Eve, 1814, but the last battle was fought at New Orleans in February, 1815, again due to inadequate communications. In British history, the war has been completely over-shadowed by the final victory over Napoleon in 1815 at Waterloo. In the United States, it is still remembered in a somewhat romantic way as, for example, by the Society of Veterans of the War of 1812. In Canada, it is remembered mainly because of incidents such as the death of General Brock and the journey of Laura Secord, prior to the battle of Beaverdams (near the route of the Welland Canal), as well as by such notable victories as those at Chateauguay (Quebec) and Crysler's Farm (Ontario), two locations close to the Seaway of today.

Generally unrecognized, however, is the fact that the War of 1812 exercised a profound influence upon the building of canals in Canada. The start of the building of the Lachine Canal was an indirect result. More direct was the specific defence requirement of an alternative route to that up the St. Lawrence between Montreal and Kingston, the bastion at the exit from Lake Ontario, important also as a naval base and naval ship-building establishment. Throughout the years of war, all naval and military personnel and all supplies and munitions bound for Kingston had to be transported laboriously up or around the rapids of the St. Lawrence. In the international section of the River (between Lake St. Francis and Lake Ontario), this critical supply line was in constant danger of ambush from the U.S. bank of the River. Some forays did take place and one small flotilla was lost.

British commanders were well aware of this ever-present danger. U.S. commanders were equally aggrieved by their inability to attack more supply outfits due to lack of access by land to their bank of the St. Lawrence. Even before the end of the War, appeals were made to the British Government for immediate study of an alternative route. Officers of the Royal Engineers made the necessary surveys and confirmed that such a route did exist — starting up the Ottawa River from Ste -Anne, with canals built around three rapids, the greatest being the Long Sault of the Ottawa (near the Hawkesbury of today). The Rideau River, from near the Chaudière Falls on the Ottawa River up into the Rideau Lakes, would have to be made navigable by constructing canals around all its rapids. Similarly, the rapids on the Cataraqui River would have to be by-passed and a connection made between the two rivers through the Lakes.

Through the initiative of one of the greatest of Canada's early Governors, the fourth Duke of Richmond, a modest start was made in 1819 at the building of the Grenville Canal, one of the three small Ottawa River Canals. During the summer of 1819, the Duke inspected the route of the Rideau Canal (on horseback and on foot) but died tragically in the course of this journey from rabies, following a bite by a pet fox. Had he lived, a start would surely have been made at building the Rideau Canal, but nothing more was then done. The Duke had planned to complete his journey down the Ottawa River, visiting the start of the Grenville Canal. Following his death, the work continued slowly. Only after the British Government had received the Report of a Commission of Inquiry, headed by Colonel Sir James Carmichael Smythe, late in 1825 was the decision made to prosecute actively these extensive works.

The Ottawa River Canals were built by the little-known Royal Staff Corps of the British Army (and not by the Royal Engineers as popularly supposed), under the command of Lt. Col. Henry du Vernet. Contractors were employed when a very late start was made on the Chute

à Blondeau and Carillon Canals but the six-mile Grenville Canal, involving 480,000 cubic yards of rock excavation, all done by hand, was built by direct labour under the RSC officers. Due to readily explainable delays, the three little canals were opened only at the start of the 1834 navigation season. The three upstream locks on the Grenville Canal (built before 1825) were made to the same dimensions as those on the early Lachine Canal, 100 feet long by 20 feet wide. They should have been rebuilt to the dimensions of all the other locks on the system (134 feet long and 34 feet wide). But this was not done and so the bottleneck of Canada's first Seaway was provided by the upper three locks on the Grenville Canal, much to the chagrin of the great Duke of Wellington who was keenly aware of the vital defence importance of the Ottawa-Rideau route.

The Rideau Canal, with its 47 locks and 52 impounding dams, was built by the Royal Engineers under the command of Lt. Col. John By. Contractors were used for the building of all major structures. Started in a small way in September 1826, the Canal was opened throughout its full length of 123 miles in May 1832. Even by modern construction standards this would be a fine record. For the early nineteenth century, and with no mechanical plant available, all work being done by hand, it was a superb achievement. But, while following his instructions to get this military work completed with all despatch, Colonel By slightly exceeded the expenditure authorized by the British Parliament (by £88,000). He was recalled to face a Parliamentary Committee of Inquiry and, although exonerated, did not receive the honours so justly his due and died four years after his return to England.

These details of canals other than those along the St. Lawrence may appear irrelevant

Top
Brockville in 1828 as seen across the St. Lawrence, by James Gray.

Bottom
The "Battle of Windmill Point" (near Prescott); 1838, by Salathiel Ellis.

to the story of the Seaway. Far from it, since at the time that the Ottawa-Rideau system was opened (1834), it *was* the Seaway. Not until the completion in 1851 of the last of the initial St. Lawrence Canals would vessels be able to sail directly up the St. Lawrence into Lake Ontario from the ocean-connected river at Montreal. For the period 1834 to 1851, the regular military and commercial route from Montreal to the Great Lakes was therefore by way of the Ottawa River and Rideau Canals. Regular freight and passenger services were operated. Military supplies and small naval vessels, naturally free of tolls, used this alternative route, as originally intended under the alarms of war. And some small vessels did come up from the Atlantic Ocean and transit into Lake Ontario, thus marking the beginning of that direct connection between the oceans and the Great Lakes that is today so splendidly provided by the Seaway.

These developments were known and appreciated across the border in the United States. There "canal mania" was in full swing, soon to be eclipsed by "railroad mania", exactly as would happen also in Europe. One of the grandest and most imaginative projects in New York State was for a canal linking the Hudson River at Albany with the Great Lakes. First proposed

Prescott as seen from Ogdens- 19
burgh in 1840, by **W.H. Bart-**
lett.

in 1807, this canal was always envisaged as connecting the Hudson River with Lake Erie, and not Lake Ontario, in order to divert all possible traffic from the West to the American route to New York and away from the Canadian route down the St. Lawrence to Montreal. The "Erie Canal" was its popular name and it was built by De Witt Clinton. The War of 1812 delayed its start until 1817; it was finished in 1825. Rebuilt later, and now a part of the New York State Barge Canal system, it still performs useful service for moderate sized vessels. The threat which its completion in 1825 presented to the flow of traffic down the St. Lawrence was very

largely responsible for the building of yet another of the precursors of the Seaway of today, the first Welland Canal.

The First
Welland Canal

THE NIAGARA Peninsula was the one great obstacle to navigation on the Great Lakes. Sailing from Lake Erie into Lake Huron and thence into Lake Michigan presented no serious problems for early shallow-draft vessels. The St. Mary's Rapids had to be passed in order to gain access to Lake Superior but a simple portage road with a rise of only twenty feet made the transfer relatively easy. The first small lock was built here (by the North West Company) in 1797-98. Today, the great locks at Sault Ste. Marie handle over one hundred million tons of freight every year. But the passage from Lake Ontario into Lake Erie was a different matter. The difference in water level between the two lakes is 327 feet. Niagara Falls, known around the world, accounts for about three fifths only of this great fall (or rise), the remainder evidenced by the swift flowing water and rapids both above and below the great Falls. On land, the Niagara Escarpment, so dominant a feature of the landscape of southwestern Ontario, accounts for much of the rise, the land below and above the Escarpment being relatively level.

Laborious portaging of canoes and their loads over simple trails had at first to suffice. As the portage roads were improved, the use of separate fleets of small vessels in the two lakes was a logical development, cargoes alone being portaged. One of the earliest of marine railways was installed in the mid-eighteenth century, operated by a capstan at the top of the Escarpment. Small bateaux could be hauled up in this way, being transported along simple roads from

William Hamilton Merritt; the statue honouring him in St. Catharines.

navigable water to and from the bottom and top of the incline. The fact that such a high toll as £10 (New York currency) was charged for this transfer is a good indication of its value to early transportation between the Lakes. Small wonder that the idea of a canal across the Peninsula became a continuing dream.

One of the earliest records of the idea of a canal is contained in a report made to the French king, Louis XIV, which rightly said that a canal could be built only at very great expense. It was not until the start of the nineteenth century that any serious consideration was given to the idea. William Hamilton Merritt — promoter and builder of the first Welland Canal — once said that the idea of the canal came to him in the year 1812 "when riding along the Niagara River to the Chippawa Ferry". It was not until 1818 that he made his first survey of a possible route for a canal to feed water from the Welland River to his mill on Twelve Mile Creek. It is now clear that the building of the Erie Canal led to the extension of this simple concept into that of a navigable canal linking Lakes Ontario and Erie.

The first of several petitions to the Legislature of Upper Canada, in October 1818, mentions specifically the competition for Canadian trade to be expected from the new Erie Canal. It was not until 18 May 1823 that the Legislature finally passed an Act incorporating the Welland Canal Company, Merritt naturally being one of the incorporators. The necessary capital was raised, but with difficulty, appeal having to be made to the Legislature for help, and finally to the British Government which provided a loan of £55,555. This indicated the defence significance attached to the Canal and may well have been made at the instigation of the Duke of Wellington. The Duke had himself taken out 25 shares in the Company; their later sale provided the fund from which the Wellington scholarships of Trinity College in the University of Toronto are still paid today.

Despite all difficulties, including mistakes by contractors and serious trouble with the final stage of excavation of the Big Cut (between present-day Allanburg and Port Robinson), the canal was finally completed. It included no less than 40 locks, 100 feet long and 22 feet wide with seven feet of water over their sills. With a long flight of such simple structures, all built of timber, a water connection was provided up and over the great Escarpment, initially to the Welland River, and only later directly into Lake Erie at Port Colborne. This original connection to the tributary of the Niagara River probably explains why "Welland" was adopted for the name of the new canal, instead of "Niagara", as might have been expected. The very idea of thus conveying vessels by water up and down the more than 300 feet between the Lakes is today an indication of inspired imagination and high courage. But the task was done, and on 20 November 1829, two schooners were successfully conveyed from Lake Ontario to Lake Erie — almost exactly 150 years ago from the date of publication of this volume.

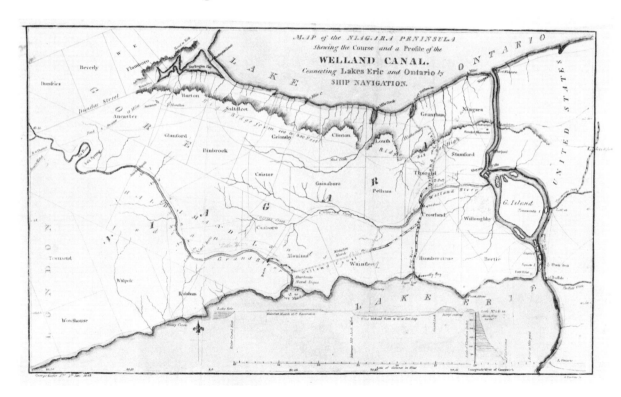

A map of the first Welland Canal, drawn in 1828 by G. Keefer Jr.

24 *An early view on the Welland Canal.*

In the Deep Cut of the second Welland Canal.

The second Welland Canal near St. Catharines.

Entrance to the Welland Canal at Port Colborne. 27

The First St. Lawrence Canals

BELOW LAKE Ontario, the little "Engineer Canals" continued their limited service in the Soulanges section of the St. Lawrence, but the Long Sault of the St. Lawrence (near Cornwall) continued as a mass of white water, passable only by laboriously unloading upward-bound vessels, portaging passengers and freight and hauling up the empty vessels with ropes. Word of the successful completion and operation of the new Welland Canal undoubtedly reached early settlers in the Cornwall area. They certainly knew of the Ottawa and Rideau Canals and their potential for through service between Montreal and Kingston. It was, therefore, no mere coincidence that, in the same year in which the complete Ottawa-Rideau route was finally opened (1834), the Government of Upper Canada made a start on the construction of the first Cornwall Canal,

28 *The Long Sault of the St. Lawrence and excavation for the first Cornwall Canal in progress in 1840, by W.H. Bartlett.*

to circumvent the great rapids of the Long Sault. The Canal had to be eleven miles long with six locks, 200 feet long by 45 feet wide with nine feet of water over the sills — the increased size of the locks being an indication of the rapid growth in the dimensions of steamboats. Inadequate financing resulted in very slow progress on the Canal, all work being stopped at the time of the "troubles" in 1837, to be resumed only in 1842. Completion came in 1843.

The British Government in 1839 appointed the Earl of Durham as the new Governor of Canada with wide powers of inquiry to review the critical problems of British North America, evidenced by the uprisings of 1837. His stay in Canada was curtailed to five months only, but such was his appreciation of the overall situation that the Report which he rendered early in 1840 provided the foundation for the self-government which was soon to be featured not only in Canada, but in all other parts of the British Commonwealth. Unfortunately, some of his remarks about Canadians were indiscreet, at the very least, and still give offence to many. This has unfortunately tended to overshadow the constructive part of the great Report, from which all Canadians would ultimately benefit, and also the wide-ranging sweep of his studies. He saw

Another early view of the Long Sault, showing a steamboat (left) in the completed Cornwall Canal in 1849.

29

clearly the importance of water transportation to the future of Canada and commissioned a special report on this subject from an officer of the Royal Engineers, Lt. Col. George Phillpotts. This officer presented his report, another outstanding document, early in 1840 but so sudden had been Lord Durham's departure from Canada that he was unable to use the recommendations of Colonel Phillpotts in his own Report.

The Phillpotts Report was eventually published, in part. It contains a ringing endorsement of the St. Lawrence route as the commercial waterway to the Great Lakes, while appreciating the continuing defence significance of the Ottawa-Rideau route. The approach taken by Colonel Phillpotts is well illustrated by these few words from the first part of his Report:

> Unless we open an uninterrupted navigation for large steamers capable of carrying a cargo of at least 300 tons without transhipment before they arrive at Montreal or Quebec, we have no chance whatever of securing any great portion of that vast and important trade which must ere long be carried on between the Western States and the Atlantic Ocean.

Upper and Lower Canada were combined into the United Province of Canada in 1841, in line with Lord Durham's suggestions. One of the first actions under the new administration of

30 *Lock No. 2 of the Beauharnois Canal; the Soulanges Canal replaced this Canal.*

Lord Sydenham was the appointment of a Board of Works to be responsible for all public works, including canals. In 1842, the British Parliament passed the Canada Loan Act and the new Legislature directed that the proceeds of this loan should be used immediately for canal construction and reconstruction, as well as for road building. Surveys were started in 1841; by 1842 an active programme of canal development was under way by the Board of Works. By 1845 the first Welland Canal had been rebuilt, its locks reduced in number from 40 to 27 and built as masonry structures, 150 feet long and 26 feet 6 inches wide. The Cornwall Canal was finally completed and work was started on the three smaller Williamsburg Canals, at Farran Point, completed in 1847; at Rapide Plat, also opened in 1847; and the Iroquois-Galop Canal, finished after some difficulty, in 1851. Downstream of Lake St. Francis were still the small "Engineer Canals". After much argument, it was decided to replace them by an entirely new canal on the south bank of the River, despite the fact that this location, so close to the United States of America, was looked upon askance by defence authorities. This new Beauharnois Canal was 11.5 miles long and had nine locks giving a total rise and fall of 82.5 feet. Started in 1842, it was

Beauharnois Canal; lock No. 9   31
at Valleyfield.

completed in 1845, a fine construction achievement for those days.

From 1851, therefore, the St. Lawrence route superseded the Ottawa-Rideau route as the waterway from Montreal to the Great Lakes. Traffic increased steadily — from 450,000 tons of freight in 1851 to 1,200,000 tons in 1870, with slightly greater tonnages passing through the Welland Canal. Traffic through the Ottawa-Rideau system was now reduced to that generated in or serving local communities. The threat of the Erie Canal, however, remained. The fact that it led to New York, an ocean port open throughout the year, gave it a decided advantage. Small wonder then, that there was continuing agitation for further improvement of the St. Lawrence and Welland Canals, once the combined system had shown its possibilities.

32 *The busy harbour of Picton, towards the end of the 19th century.*

The Fourteen-Foot Canals

THIS WAS a time of crucial political developments in Canada, culminating in the passing by the British Parliament in 1867 of the British North America Act, by which some of the British colonies in North America became the self-governing Dominion of Canada. The old Board of Works became the Department of Public Works (as it still is), now charged with wider and far-flung activities, of which canals were only a part, important as they still were. In 1871, the new Government appointed a Commission to study all the canal problems of the new Dominion. Its Report proved to be a State paper of unusual importance.

The vital character of the St. Lawrence-Welland route in the overall Canadian commercial scene was fully recognized and the general recommendation made that almost all existing canals should be rebuilt to accommodate larger

The harbour of Cobourg, showing one of the early St. Lawrence lighthouses.

Opposite
Montreal, the Victoria Bridge, the west end of Montreal Harbour, and the entrance to the Lachine Canal, photographed about 1896 by W. Notman.

A companion view, showing the Lachine Rapids in the background, the Lachine Canal going off (right) to Lake St. Louis; photo by W. Notman.

vessels, with the depth of water over the sills of all new locks to be at least 14 feet. The government accepted the recommendation and the new nation embarked upon a series of reconstructions that constituted, relatively speaking, one of the greatest programmes of public works ever carried out in Canada. Viewed with the hindsight possible today, this was the more remarkable since the great period of railroad construction was just about to begin. But the job was done, and so well done that, apart only from the Welland, the "14-foot canals" were still serving faithfully when the Seaway of today was built.

Opposite
Mail steamer Corsican *entering Montreal Harbour under the (original) Victoria Bridge after running the Lachine Rapids.*

36 *Steamer entering the Lachine Rapids from Lake St. Louis.*

Dealing with the canals consecutively as one travels upstream from Montreal, four entirely new locks were built on the Lachine Canal, adjacent to the existing locks which had to be maintained in full operation throughout the period of rebuilding, and which themselves were later rebuilt and retained as twins to the new locks. All locks measured 270 feet long by 45 feet wide, with 17 feet of water over the sills of the first two and 14 feet for the remainder. A new guard lock was built at Lachine and other major improvements made to the Canal. The necessity of keeping the Canal operating at all times explains the long period taken for reconstruction, from 1863 to 1884, but the resulting "new" Canal is that still to be seen today, although not now in use since the opening of the Seaway.

The greatest change in the reconstruction programme was the replacement of the Beauharnois Canal by an entirely new Soulanges Canal, but on the north shore of the River as were the original "Engineer Canals". It was 14.6 miles long with only five locks instead of the nine on the Beauharnois Canal, all the locks being 280 feet long by 46 feet wide with the usual depth of 14 feet over the sills. Construction of this new canal was straightforward, with no complication from traffic. It took from 1892 to 1899. The

Steamer in one of the Lachine Canal locks and (below) unloading ships at Montreal by electric light, in 1882.

A later view of shipping at the Montreal entrance to the Lachine Canal.

Cornwall Canal, on the other hand, had to be rebuilt and enlarged while being maintained in full operation and so this task took from 1876 to 1904. The new locks here were 270 feet long and 45 feet wide with the exception of Lock No. 17 which had the distinction of being only 43 feet, 8 inches wide. Between Locks 16 and 17, a water area of two acres was made available for berthing ships for repair work, and a dry dock was constructed.

The three smaller canals upstream of the Long Sault were similarly reconstructed during the same period, generally to the same lock dimensions, although advantage was taken of the

S. S. Winnipeg, a typical "14-footer".

Making the harbour of Port Hope in a storm about 1880.

A typical bridge-tender's shelter on the Lachine Canal.

40   *The south-west end of the Lachine Canal, showing the entrance from Lake St. Louis.*

opportunity to combine, in two locations, two of the locks to form "double locks" of standard width but 800 feet long. And an unusual "river lock" was provided in the Galop Canal through which downstream vessels could pass from the upper part of the Canal directly into the River, sailing down its swift waters instead of using the remaining locks, with consequent saving of time. Finally, the Welland Canal was reconstructed again — as the Third Welland Canal — between 1883 and 1887, all locks being enlarged to the standard dimensions, one only of the existing locks being eliminated, all now with 14 feet of water available over the sills.

This was the system of 14-foot St. Lawrence Canals that served Canada well, and the United States of America, until the coming of the Seaway. The system was itself a minor Seaway and several steamship companies had ocean-going vessels built to dimensions that would just enable them to use the 14-foot locks. At the end of this service, no less than 14 overseas shipping companies were using the St. Lawrence Canals in regular sailings into the Great Lakes; 120 vessels were involved. There were 225 overseas sailings from the Port of Chicago alone in 1954. For inland trade a fleet of almost 200 "14-footers" was gradually built up,

Constructing the Soulanges Canal; excavation by digging and dredging, in 1895.

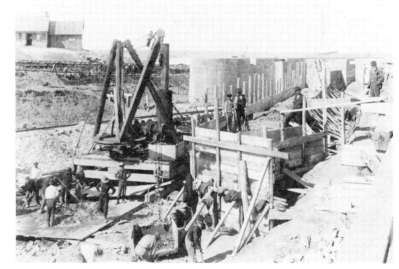

Constructing one of the lock walls for the Soulanges Canal in 1899.

sturdy, if not exactly beautiful, vessels generally 253 feet long and capable of carrying 2,800 tons of iron ore or 106,000 bushels of grain. They served well and, together with other craft, were using the St. Lawrence Canals to their maximum capacity when the service ended in 1959. Traffic had by then exceeded eleven million tons of freight per year.

A vessel about to leave the Soulanges Canal at Coteau Landing, about 1900; photo by W. Notman.

S. S. John Pratt *in a lock on the Soulanges Canal; photo by W.J. Topley.*

An aerial view of Cornwall, taken about 1920, showing the start of the 14-foot Cornwall Canal.

S. S. Algerian *descending the* Long Sault *(the Cornwall Canal being behind the photographer — W. Notman).*

43

Below left
A raft of large timbers going down the Long Sault near the end of the 19th century; photo by D.D. Calvin.

Below right
Morrisburg as seen from the air in the early 1920s, with the start of the Morrisburg 14-foot canal.

Sailing vessels at the Port Colborne entrance to the Welland Canal, about 1885.

The "River Lock" on the Galop 14-foot canal, through which downbound vessels could enter the River.

44

An early aerial view of Port Dalhousie, entrance to the third Welland Canal from Lake Ontario.

The third Welland Canal near Thorold, part of the 14-foot canal system.

46   S. S. Fairlake, *another typical "14-footer" upward bound in the Lachine Canal.*

The Proposed Georgian Bay Ship Canal

THROUGHOUT THE long period of development of the St. Lawrence Canals, residents of the Ottawa Valley continued in their belief that it was up the Ottawa River that the Seaway would ultimately be built. This would mean providing locks on the Ottawa River around the Chaudière rapids (at Ottawa) and around all the other rapids and falls up to Mattawa, then similar control of the small Mattawa River up to and over the portage which gave connection to Lake Nipissing, and finally building locks on the French River down to Georgian Bay. This project was first proposed to Colonel By while he was building the Rideau Canal; it was to remain a topic of lively interest throughout the Valley for the next hundred years.

This route was 300 miles shorter into Lake Huron from Montreal than using the St. Lawrence. It involved, however, a rise of 659 feet from the harbour of Montreal to the summit level at Trout Lake and then a subsequent drop of 99 feet into Georgian Bay, thus necessitating more lockage than the St. Lawrence route. The shorter length compensated, to a degree, for the extra lockage, so that the two routes were directly comparable as links between the upper Great Lakes and the sea.

The first real survey of the Ottawa route was made in 1856 by Walter Shanly, an outstanding civil engineer of early Canada. This was followed by a number of other surveys and the project was the subject of many Parliamentary inquiries. In addition to the commercial possibilities of the Ottawa route, it was always viewed with special favour by British defence authorities — and defence was the last governmental responsibility to be taken over from the British by the Government of Canada. A notable journey of inspection by canoe along the entire Ottawa Waterway, from Georgian Bay to Montreal, was undertaken as late as 1865 by the respective commanding Admiral and General in British North America. And the last British defence report advocating, inter alia, the construction of the "Ottawa Seaway" was made as recently as 1912.

The "Georgian Bay Ship Canal" was the name that gradually came into use to denote the Ottawa Seaway as the nineteenth century neared its close. It was used in the title of the notable Report prepared by the Department of Public Works and presented to Parliament during the 1909 session. This splendid document gave detailed plans and estimates of cost for a real Seaway, the locks to be 600 feet long by 60 feet wide with 20 feet of water over the sills. It could be built for $100,000,000 in ten years, so it was estimated, and would have an annual maintenance bill of $900,000. Sir Wilfrid Laurier promised that if his party was returned to office in the General Election of 1911, the Georgian Bay Ship Canal would be built. But this was the "Reciprocity Election" in which the Liberal party was beaten. Laurier's promise could not be implemented and so the concept of the Ship Canal up the Ottawa gradually faded from public view, although still not forgotten even today. What effect it would have had on the entire economy of north-eastern North America can now only be imagined.

Indicative of the intense rivalry between proponents of the two competing routes was the decision that had to be made in 1911-1912 by the new Conservative Government of Sir Robert Borden. They had before them not only the Department of Public Works Report on the Ottawa route but also a detailed proposal from the Department of Railways and Canals (now responsible for all canals) for an entirely new Welland Canal, the fourth. Little is to be gained by reciting the arguments pro and con, although even today it is strange to think that the complete Seaway up the Ottawa appears to have been compared, in cost and time for completion, with just one part of the St. Lawrence Seaway, the Welland Canal. The decision was made in favour of the Welland, however, and a start made in 1913 at one of the greatest of all Canadian construction projects up to that time. And the new Welland Canal, conceived with such vision and imagination more than sixty years ago, is today a vital part of the St. Lawrence Seaway.

HOPE

D TRUNK BRIDGE

A reminder of the Ottawa Waterway; vessels under the Grand Trunk Railway bridge at Ste-Anne de Bellevue where the Ottawa joins the St. Lawrence.

49

*Start of construction of the
fourth Welland Canal in 1913.*

The Fourth Welland Canal

IT WILL be recalled that the third Welland Canal, completed in 1887, had 26 masonry locks, all on the same scale as those on the St. Lawrence Canals — 280 feet long by 46 feet wide with the usual 14 feet of water over sills. The engineers responsible for the design of the fourth Welland Canal across the Niagara Peninsula did not at-tempt any minor improvements of the existing canal but boldly contemplated a new major ship canal. Although the route chosen from the top of the Escarpment was but little different in course from that of the third canal, the entrance from Lake Erie still being at Port Colborne, a new route was selected for the canal below the Es-carpment. An entirely new entrance from Lake Ontario was planned, five miles to the east of Port Dalhousie, later to be named Port Weller. The most striking part of the new design, how-ever, was the reduction in the number of locks from 26 to seven, with a special eighth guard lock at Port Colborne, and in the gigantic size

Early stage in the construction of Port Weller on Lake Ontario, to be the new entrance for the fourth Welland Canal; in 1914.

proposed for them. As built, the new locks were 859 feet long and 80 feet wide with 30 feet of water over the sills, a far cry from the 40 little wooden locks of the original canal.

The first three of the new locks were to be individual locks with short stretches of canal intervening. Another inspired part of the design was to combine the fourth, fifth and sixth locks into a single flight, each lock in duplicate so as to permit the simultaneous movement of two vessels, one up and one down this gigantic nautical staircase. The seventh lock was another single lock leading to a long level stretch of canal finishing at the Port Colborne guard lock. This

Excavation proceeding near Thorold for the fourth Welland Canal; in 1914.

Excavation for the twin locks on the new Welland Canal, in 1916, just before work was halted.

eighth lock was of unusual length: 1200 feet long, as compared to the usable length of 765 feet for the other locks. This was engineering planning in the spirit of the nineteen seventies! Yet it was done at the time of the First World War and the canal successfully constructed in the years that followed the end of that conflict. The start in 1913 was on a modest scale indeed. Excavation work continued after the start of the war in 1914 but was eventually halted in 1917. In 1919 a new start was made, again slowly. Activity increased rapidly in the early twenties, to such good effect that the new canal was in use in 1931, the official opening taking place in the following year.

Throughout the entire construction period, the older canal was maintained in full operation, as it had to be in view of the freight that it now carried. Even during the construction period, of a decade and a half, the volume of traffic doubled to over six million tons of freight a year. Since much of the upper part of the old canal was incorporated into the new one, the relative uses of new and old channels and the arrangement of the necessary dredging and other construction operations had to be most carefully scheduled. No major difficulties were experienced, although some of the contractors responsible encountered

Construction of the twin locks under way, in 1921.

54

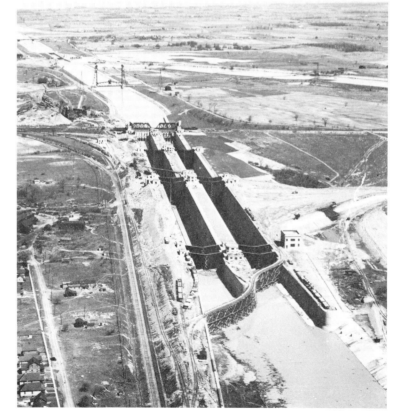

Flight locks approaching completion, in 1930, looking towards Lake Ontario.

serious problems in their work of excavating glacial till. So important was the completion of the canal considered by the Government of Canada that the official opening was postponed until August 1932 when the British Empire Economic Conference was being held in Canada. Delegates were transported from Ottawa to the Canal and in their presence on 6 August 1932 the Governor General, the Earl of Bessborough, declared the fourth Welland Canal open for use by ships of all nations, especially those of Canada and the United States of America. A new phase in navigation on the Great Lakes had begun.

It took a few years for the full effect of the

Lock No. 1, complete except for its gates and controls.

Steel framework for a lock gate under erection, its size indicated by the men to be seen.

enlarged canal to be felt but slowly yet steadily a new fleet of "upper-lakers" was built by interested steamship companies. These large vessels were approximately 600 feet long, but fitted easily into the new locks on the Welland, as they did into the newer locks at Sault Ste. Marie. Grain had previously been shipped from the head of Lake Superior to transfer points on Lake Erie but now, in increasing volume, it was conveyed by the new ships down into Lake Ontario. Coal and iron ore could similarly be brought from the upper Lakes into Lake Ontario, notably to Hamilton with its large steel plants. The Government of Canada constructed

at Prescott a large grain elevator essentially for transhipment purposes since beyond this point the upper-lakers could not sail.

The main pattern of grain shipments on the Great Lakes thus became transport in upper-lakers from Lake Superior through the locks at Sault Ste. Marie, Lake Huron, the St. Clair River, Lake Erie and the Welland Canal into Lake Ontario for unloading at Prescott. Here the stubby 14-footers would load up from the elevator and complete the transport of the grain to the elevators at Montreal, whence the final ocean sailings could be made to the markets of the world. Despite the years of economic depres-

Vessel crossing the new Welland Canal, 1928.

Lock No. 8, at Port Colborne, approaching completion in 1928.

sion, traffic through the new Welland Canal increased from almost nine million tons a year at its opening to over 27 million tons in 1959, in large part due to shipments of grain.

Final dredging in progress in Port Colborne Harbour; in 1929.

Steam vessels ("14-footers") waiting at Port Dalhousie in 1928 to get into the partially completed new Welland Canal.

S. S. Lemoyne *at the official opening of the fourth Welland Canal, 6 August 1932.*

The Modern Seaway

THE BOTTLENECK formed by the St. Lawrence River Canals remained, however, despite the obvious success of the greatly enlarged Welland Canal. Small ocean vessels continued their service across the Atlantic into the Great Lakes but their limited size inevitably made their contribution to international trade a small one. The years of the Second World War emphasized in no uncertain manner not only the serious impediment that the "14-foot bottleneck" constituted, but also the economic loss of allowing the long-recognized power potential of the Long Sault and the rapids above (more than two million horse power) to remain undeveloped. Development of the power potential of the all-Canadian Soulanges section of the St. Lawrence (almost two million horse power) had been achieved at Beauharnois in 1932. Both downstream and upstream of the International Section of the River, therefore, great civil engineering works in Canada from 1932 onwards showed what could be achieved. Opposition to corresponding works in the International Section was, however, long-standing and powerful.

As early as 1895 the Governments of Canada and the United States jointly appointed a Deep Waterways Commission, charged with a study of all possible routes between the Great Lakes and the sea. Competition between the Erie Canal and the St. Lawrence route, as well as the proposed Georgian Bay Ship Canal, was then very much in the air. The Commission reported in 1897 in favour of improving the St. Lawrence route, and from that date started the opposition to any such joint undertaking. It grew more recalcitrant with time. Those opposed included, quite naturally, the railroads, the Atlantic coast ports, ports in Texas, and also (surprisingly) some cities of the mid-West, all banded together in the National St. Lawrence Project Conference, a body more accurately described by its subtitle — a Nation-wide Organization in Opposition.

The power potential of the International Section had been recognized since the first years of the century. In 1909, as a development of the earlier Commission, Canada and the U.S.A. signed a treaty establishing the International

Dredging the power canal at Beauharnois, in 1931, the power house in the background, the canal later to be used also as part of the Seaway.

59

Joint Commission which, thereafter, was responsible for all studies of power and navigation on the St. Lawrence, as well as for all other boundary water questions. Applications for private development of the St. Lawrence power were made in 1918 and 1921 but were not granted. Political developments in both countries led to the power project becoming the responsibility of the Province of Ontario and the State of New York. Joint Boards of Engineers laboured through the years, preparing and refining plans for the most efficient use of the International Section, always with both power generation and deep-water navigation in view (the latter made possible by the damming of the River for power). Power development was at first contemplated in two stages, with two power houses, but with significant advances in civil engineering practice (notably in the engineering use of soils) it was eventually possible to design a single stage development with one power house, two large locks serving to raise or lower vessels through the full head utilized in the turbines.

The opposition continued unabated. Even though a treaty covering a two-stage development with associated locks was signed by both countries in 1932, it failed to win the necessary two thirds majority vote in the Senate of the United States and so was inoperative. The arguments continued. Not until 1946, when the suggestion was first advanced of charging tolls for the use of the Seaway, with the object of making it self-supporting, was there any hope of progress. The decision to develop actively the iron ore deposits of Labrador, at about the same time, proved to be a decisive factor, as did also the urgent post-war power demands in Ontario and New York for utilization of the two million horse power still going to waste down the Long Sault.

Finally, the Prime Minister of Canada, Mr. Louis St. Laurent, in a meeting with President Harry Truman in the White House in September 1951, made it quite clear that Canada was prepared to go ahead to build, on its own and at its own expense, the new navigation facilities in association with the building of the international power house by Ontario and New York. Action followed, although still impeded by appeals all the way up to the Supreme Court of the United States. At last, on 13 May 1954, the necessary legislation was passed by the U.S. Congress. An exchange of Notes followed as quickly as possible, defining the respective responsibilities of each country. Construction of the Seaway could start at last. The engineers of both countries were ready. The first sod was turned near Cornwall, with all due ceremony, on 10 August 1954.

Building the Seaway

FOUR GOVERNMENTAL agencies were responsible for design and construction, always under the watchful eye of the International Joint Commission, and subject to the ultimate authority of their respective governments. The Hydro Electric Power Commission of Ontario and the Power Authority of the State of New York were jointly responsible for the power development. Their work had to be completely integrated with that of the two navigation agencies, the St. Lawrence Seaway Authority in Canada (a Crown Corporation) and the Saint Lawrence Seaway Development Corporation in the United States. All costs of the power development were shared equally, since the ancillary works in both countries necessitated by the flooding of lands upstream of the power house were naturally a joint responsibility. Costs for the navigation facilities were shared proportionally, the cost of the improvements required at the fourth Welland Canal being allowed for in the negotiations. The total cost of all navigation and power facilities approximated one billion dollars.

This vast expenditure was spent in five years, a phenomenally short time for the prosecution of so great a project, with works extending throughout the 190 miles from Montreal to Lake Ontario. By way of comparison, it took ten years to construct the Suez Canal, with no locks, and 22 years for the Panama Canal. Over 500 professional engineers were at work at the peak of the design activity of the four main agencies alone. Many other agencies were involved, directly and indirectly, in parts of the work. As but two examples of many, Hydro Quebec was involved with all the works impinging on the Beauharnois power development; and Canadian National Railways with the relocation of 20 miles of their main line west of Cornwall, and with the "twinning" of the Victoria Bridge at its southern end. At one time no less than 22,000 men were at work between Montreal and Lake Ontario, all engaged on integrated parts of the overall project.

The grand design, as is so often the case, was simple in overall concept, but complex in its myriad details. The new canal was located from Montreal to Lake St. Louis on the south bank of the River, the drop in the Lachine Rapids taken up in two locks, at St. Lambert and Côte Ste-Catherine. The dredged channel across the Lake led to two locks in tandem at the west end of the Beauharnois power house. The power canal was used, after dredging, as the navigation channel up to Lake St. Francis. By mutual agreement the channel and locks in the International Section were located on the south bank of the River, and so were the responsibility of the U.S. Seaway agency. Two locks were necessary, located in a ten-mile-long newly excavated channel. The power house and a major spillway dam raised the water level to flood what had been the Long Sault and the smaller rapids above. At the head of this section, another control dam was located at Iroquois with an associated control lock in Canada, the dam built by the U.S. power agency and the lock by the Canadian Seaway Authority. And across Lake Ontario the fourth Welland Canal finally took its place as an integral part of the complete Seaway.

The size of the existing locks on the Welland Canal was a decisive factor in the solution of one of the major design policy questions — what size should the Seaway locks be? They were built essentially to the same dimensions as those on the Welland Canal — 800 feet long (765 feet usable) and 80 feet wide with 30 feet of water over the sills; channels were dredged initially to a depth of 25 feet only. With the construction of the Seaway in the 1950s, they were deepened to 27 feet. Indicative of the type of design problems that had to be faced was the whole question of clearances under the bridges that crossed the Seaway. The lift bridges over the Welland Canal already provided the necessary clearance, as did the bridge across the St. Lawrence River at Ivy Lea, a reminder of far-sighted planning. Bridges at Cornwall had to be replaced by two bridges for highway traffic, an earlier railroad bridge having fallen into disuse. At Beauharnois, the bridges across the power canal had all been designed, back in 1930, so that their central spans could one day be replaced by lift spans when the Seaway was built and the canal used also for navigation. Replacement of these spans was a straightforward job, as was also the construction of a vehicular tunnel for the main highway crossing at the Beauharnois locks.

The highway and railroad bridges at the Montreal end of the Seaway presented some of the most complex but interesting of all the design and construction problems. All bridges had to be kept in full operating condition while ad-

62 *Start of construction of the St. Lambert Lock, Montreal, first lock on the Seaway; 8 June 1956.*

justed appropriately to give the necessary clearance over the water level in the new navigation channel. The Honoré Mercier and Jacques Cartier highway bridges were jacked up by small increments, steadily increasing to a maximum at the spans over the Seaway. Some piers of the southern section of the Jacques Cartier bridge, for example, were thus increased in height by a maximum of 50 feet, the key span itself being replaced by a new through truss span built alongside and slid into place in six hours, this being the only period during which the bridge was closed to traffic throughout its major reconstruction.

Perhaps the most interesting of all the special problems was the building of the St. Lambert lock adjacent to the venerable Victoria Bridge which carried the main line of Canadian National Railways to south and east as well as an important and busy highway. This bridge, the piers of which date from 1860, carried at one time more than 120 trains daily in addition to heavy vehicular traffic. It could not be raised and had to be kept open without interruption not only during the construction period but also after the Seaway was in operation. The elegant solution to the problem is best appreciated from photographs but, in brief, a duplicate bridge for

The setting of the St. Lambert 63
Lock, looking across the River to the Island of Montreal, the lock adjacent to the Victoria Bridge; 19 July 1956.

the last seven southern spans was built, starting with a junction with the existing bridge and then swinging westward until it was in alignment with the upstream end of the lock, another curve to the east bringing the duplicate line back to another junction with the original tracks; lift spans for the dual traffic were naturally installed for the crossings of the two lock approaches. When in operation for the passage of a westbound vessel, all traffic is diverted on to the new bridge while the downstream lift bridge is raised to allow the vessel to enter the lock. While it is being locked up, the downstream lift span is lowered through inter-locking controls, traffic is diverted back on to the original tracks and highway, and the upstream lift span is raised. The channel is then clear for the vessel to leave the lock as soon as it has been raised to the upper water level. The sequence of operation is reversed for eastbound ships, thus maintaining continuous ship, train and vehicular traffic.

Equally interesting, but on a different scale, was the control of the full flow of the River for the associated power project, while the Cornwall-Massena power house was being built. The presence of Barnhart Island, coupled with the well regulated flow of the St. Lawrence (there being no major spring flood as on other Canadian

Opposite page
Work went on day and night; a view on 13 May 1957.

A progress view of work on the St. Lambert Lock on 24 July 1957.

65

rivers) permitted the northern main channel to be closed off by a large cofferdam. The disappearance of the raging waters of the Long Sault revealed a river bed covered with massive boulders. Another cofferdam, downstream of the power house, permitted the entire structure to be built "in the dry". Throughout this period, the old Cornwall 14-foot canal continued in operation since no interference with the 14-foot service was possible. During the same period, the lands that would be flooded when the water level was raised (20,000 acres in Canada; 18,000 acres in the U.S.A.) had to be cleared, roads and railways relocated, and in Canada,

Opposite page
Traffic on the Victoria Bridge had to be maintained, despite the proximity of the Lock to piers of the Bridge; 21 August 1957.

Below left
The entrance to the Seaway as seen from the Victoria Bridge, during construction; the Jacques Cartier Bridge in the distance is being raised; 30 April 1958.

Below right
The Locks at Beauharnois, looking upstream, the power and navigation canal in the background.

Below right
Downward bound ocean freighter leaving the lower Beauharnois Lock.

Below left
Beauharnois Locks looking downstream, the power house to be seen on the right with Lake St. Louis in the background.

seven long-established riverside towns had to be replaced by three new towns. The necessary co-ordination of the scheduling of the many operations can best be left to the imagination.

Such was the speed of construction and the efficiency of the overall planning that, with the harmonious co-operation of all the agencies involved, the year 1958 saw the "beginning of the end". The dam and lock at Iroquois had actually been completed by the end of 1957; the *CGS Grenville* traversed the lock on 22 November of that year, the first vessel to use any part of the new Seaway. At 8:00 a.m. on 1st July 1958, a large charge of nitrone was detonated. This ex-

plosion breached the large cofferdam above what had been the Long Sault, allowing water to reach the power house structure. The water quickly rose to its new elevated water level (almost the same as the level of Lake Ontario). Only four days later the first generating unit was producing power. All units were gradually brought "on line"; the full output of the power house was needed by Ontario and New York as soon as it became available. By 4 July 1958, the two U.S. Locks were also ready for use and so the old 14-foot canal system passed into history, much of it now covered by "Lake St. Lawrence" as the new flooded area has been called.

Left
An aerial view of the St. Lambert Lock complex with the Jacques Cartier Bridge and the City of Montreal in the background.

Below left
Rail and road crossing of the St. Lambert Lock.

Below right
A night view of the St. Lambert Lock in use.

The Seaway channel below Côte Ste.-Catherine Lock, the Honoré Mercier Highway Bridge and the C.P.R. rail bridge in the background, Caughnawaga on the right.

Pleasure craft, bound for EXPO '67, in the St. Lambert Lock.

A vessel upward-bound leaving Côte Ste.-Catherine Lock.

All major works were completed during the following winter so that the entire Seaway was ready for use at the opening of the 1959 navigation season. The first vessel to enter the St. Lambert lock on 25 April was the *CGS d'Iberville* (one of Canada's largest ice-breakers) carrying an official party. The Royal Yacht *Britannia* sailed into this lock on 26 June following, carrying H.M. Queen Elizabeth II and President Eisenhower for the official opening. This was followed by a naval review on Lake St. Louis, and a further ceremony at the Cornwall-Massena power house (the President's place now taken by the Vice-President). A large plaque was unveiled at the ceremony; it carries words which will bring this account to a close.

Ocean-going freighter on its way to the sea, leaving the Snell Lock.

Above
Construction was proceeding simultaneously throughout the length of the Seaway; this is what the bed of the Long Sault looked like, when drained, with the Cornwall Canal, still in operation, in the background.

Left
An international waterway indeed; proof in these "graffiti" painted by sailors from vessels tied up at this wharf while waiting to go through the adjacent lock

C.G.S. d'Iberville *and* C.G.S.
Montcalm, *the first vessels to
enter the St. Lambert Lock, on
25 April 1959.*

The Royal Yacht Britannia,
*carrying H. M. The Queen and
the President, entering St.
Lambert Lock.*

H.M. The Queen and President Eisenhower met at the St. Lambert Lock for the joint Official opening of the Seaway on 26 June 1959.

H. M. The Queen unveiling the plaque at the Cornwall— Massena Power House with the Vice-President of the United States.

Above right
A large lake freighter approaching the Eisenhower Lock, the River and its islands in the background.

Above left
A Polish freighter in the Eisenhower Lock, accompanied by two smaller craft.

The viewing stand for interested visitors at the Eisenhower Lock, as seen from the deck of a freighter loaded with containers.

The Iroquois Lock looking downstream, the old 14-foot Canal to be seen in the background.

Below left
Large lake freighter in the Iroquois Lock, as seen from the control tower.

Below right
Looking upstream at the Iroquois Lock, the Prescott-Ogdensburg Bridge in the distance.

A general view of the International Section of the St. Lawrence, Cornwall and the entrance to the now abandoned 14-foot canal on the right, the Cornwall-Massena power house in the middle distance, and (in the United States) the Wiley-Dondero Canal and its two locks on the left.

76

The Seaway In Use

THE ST. LAWRENCE Seaway was now complete, one hundred and sixty years after Sir Alexander Mackenzie's prophetic statement mentioned at the outset of this account. Operation of the Seaway is the joint responsibility of the two Seaway corporations. It is now aided by modern communications systems. The positions of vessels in the Montreal to Lake Ontario section are plotted by traffic controllers in the St. Lambert traffic control centre, based on information received from canal stations and radio communications from vessels. The positions of vessels in the Welland Canal are similarly plotted by traffic controllers located in the control centre near the Flight Locks of the Canal. Controllers also observe vessel movements in certain locations along the Canal by means of closed-circuit television. The responsibility of the Seaway corporations does not extend beyond Lake Erie but considerable dredging of channels (as in the St. Clair River, for example) was an essential supplement to the Seaway proper. At Sault Ste. Marie the old Canadian lock and the four U.S. locks give access to Lake Superior, three of the U.S. locks having dimensions somewhat greater than those of the Seaway, two of them having 31 feet of water over their sills. The deep waterway, a dream in the minds of so many for so many years, now existed from the sea to the centre of the North American continent.

As the Seaway started its successful operation, the little 14-footers continued in use, but their small size soon rendered them uneconomical and they gradually disappeared from the scene, to be replaced by increasingly larger lake freighters, culminating in the magnificent "730s". These vessels are of the maximum length permissible in the Seaway locks and are 76 feet wide (only four feet less than the width of the locks). There was only one such vessel in 1959, but five in 1960. In 1978 there were over 50. This is reflected in the fact that, although traffic along the Seaway between Montreal and Lake Ontario increased from 20.6 million in 1959 to 63.3 million tons in 1977, the number of transits of vessels carrying this freight decreased from over seven thousand to less than five thousand. Similarly for the Welland Canal,

The opening of the Seaway marked the beginning of the end for the fleet of sturdy "14-footers".

A corner of the harbour of Hamilton, now an ocean port.

freight increased from 27.5 million tons in 1959 to 71.7 million tons in 1977, transits of vessels decreasing from over 8,000 to slightly more than 5,000 for the same years. It is of interest to compare these figures with corresponding statistics for the Panama Canal, so much more widely known if only because of recent political developments. In 1977 there were 12,758 transits of vessels, carrying 137.8 million tons of freight, during the twelve months of operation, figures which speak for themselves.

The Seaway has served well since its opening, with few serious interruptions. Fog on the river occasionally requires that all traffic be

Ships from the Seven Seas.

halted since even with the most sophisticated aids to navigation, safety demands visibility for ship movements on the Seaway. Some groundings of vessels have occurred, with infrequent delays to other shipping. Winter conditions present their own hazards at the opening and closing of each navigation season; the "rush to get out to the sea" as the end of each season approaches usually attracts attention in the news media. Throughout the twenty years of service, essential maintenance has been faithfully carried out, to a minor degree during open navigation but more generally after navigation has closed for the year. The Seaway Authority's

Self-unloading lake freighter starting to unload its cargo in the harbour of Oshawa.

The Port of Toronto, used by large ocean freighters.

giant floating crane, the *VM/S Hercules*, assists in this essential work.

One major improvement has been effected. A study made in 1965 showed that the part of the Welland Canal which bisected the City of Welland was crowded by city development and existing structures such as vertical lift-bridges and a railway swing bridge with a mid-canal concrete pier. A decision was therefore made to construct a new channel in an almost straight line from Port Robinson to Ramey's Bend. Many other factors supported this decision. Not only was the old channel narrow and winding but it had also become too hazardous for the ever-

increasing size of the vessels using it. The steady increase in traffic likewise increased the "up-time" of all the lift bridges, creating serious automobile traffic jams in downtown Welland. Two tunnels were therefore constructed "in the dry" beneath the new cut and all roads and railway lines were rerouted through them.

Transits of vessels through the Canal had increased to almost 30 a day. Since passage through the Canal takes between 13 and 14 hours, a reduction of this period by even half an hour is of real economic significance. Such a saving was achieved by this "Welland By-pass", built between 1967 and 1973 at a cost of $188

VM/S Hercules *lifting a lock gate.*

80

*Vessels passing in the Twin
Locks.*

million. It is 8.3 miles long with a navigable width of 350 feet. The work involved some unusual construction problems but was successfully completed and officially opened for use in an appropriate ceremony on 14 July 1973, this time in the presence of members of the Permanent International Association of Navigation Congresses, then meeting in Canada.

The Twin Locks of the Welland Canal at night.

In the upper left hand corner, a
vessel is to be seen leaving Lock
No. 7 and approaching a
paper plant in Thorold,
around which other vessels are
berthed; the Canal continues
in centre foreground.

84

Large lake freighters berthed
above Lock No. 8 at Port Colborne.

Left
The southern end of the new Welland By-pass under construction.

Below left
The final plug being removed from the end of the By-pass.

85

Below right
M. V. Griffith *in Welland Canal By-pass over East Main Street Tunnel.*

Inflation has created financial problems for the two Seaway corporations over the years since it did not prove possible to increase tolls in pace with general price increases until 1978 when a revised agreement on tolls was accepted by the two countries. To further the use of the waterway, the open season for navigation is being extended to the maximum possible extent with present facilities. Studies are being made of the possibility of extending it still further with improved facilities. The question of a longer season will be determined by its cost in relation to the benefits expected.

A longer season adds to the full capacity of

The traffic control room for the operation of the Welland Canal.

C.G.S. Ernest Lapointe, *one of Canada's icebreakers, at work in the Seaway channel below Côte Ste -Catherine Lock, looking downstream.*

the system and this capacity is rapidly being reached. An interesting experiment is in progress to determine whether a Marine Shunter system would increase the capacity of the Welland Canal. This experiment consists of two test floating platforms (rudimentary tugs), fitted with propulsion and steering components which, when attached fore and aft to vessels, will provide the motive power and control to move the vessels through the canal. If successful, the experiment will provide a means of coping with increasing demand and allow deferment until after the year 2000 of a decision to build a new canal with larger and even fewer locks. The Marine

Shunters would improve several aspects of performance by decreasing lock entry and exit times, normalizing lock performance, eliminating meeting restrictions and making navigation safer in reduced visibility.

The tremendous growth in cargo tonnage has borne out the dreams of the early planners. But the Seaway cannot stand still. The studies for an extended season and the Marine Shunter test programme are attempts to increase capacity to cope with this ever-increasing growth.

* * *

The last boat out!

December operation at St. Lambert Lock.

"Our canals were not built for Canada, but for the *Valley of the St. Lawrence*; we ought therefore, to 'club together' with our neighbours, on the opposite side in order to place this noble outlet in the most efficient state, by giving it as large a support as possible". These words were written in the year 1850 by Thomas Coltrin Keefer, another of Canada's eminent early engineers, and the italics are his. How well Canada and the United States of America have "clubbed together" on the St. Lawrence in the development of the Seaway and Power Project is now happily known throughout the world. Their joint efforts were recognized in many ways, one of the most pleasing coming in 1960 when the American Society of Civil Engineers designated the Project as the Outstanding Civil Engineering work of that year. How far away the conflict of 1812 seems as one views the Seaway today, operated jointly by two neighbour nations and used by large vessels under many flags from around the seven seas.

The hall-mark of this great work is to be found in the words engraved in gold on the fine plaque which marks the international boundary on the downstream side of the Cornwall-Massena power house — words which Her Majesty the Queen read as, with the Vice-President of the United States, she unveiled the plaque on that happy day in June 1959, words which should be known to every Canadian, these words:

THIS STONE BEARS WITNESS TO THE COMMON PURPOSE OF TWO NATIONS WHOSE FRONTIERS ARE THE FRONTIERS OF FRIENDSHIP, WHOSE WAYS ARE THE WAYS OF FREEDOM, AND WHOSE WORKS ARE THE WORKS OF PEACE.

88

89

Acknowledgments

The St. Lawrence Seaway Authority acknowledges gratefully the provision of illustrations for this volume by the following organizations, and records its thanks for permission to reproduce them:

Archives of Ontario:

Pages 44 top (S 6490); 44 middle (S 5857); 54 left (S 4195); 56 left (S 4222); and 57 top (S 4215).

Canada Wide Photos Ltd:

Pages 72 left, 73 left, 80, 86 bottom, and 87 left.

Hamilton Harbour Commissioners:

Page 78 left.

National Film Board:

Pages 67 right (88722); 69 top left (63-4815); 69 bottom left (66-14018); 69 right (66-14092); 70 top (88717); 75 top (63-9369); 75 bottom right (63-9371); 77 (92969); 78 right (66-14122); 81 (66-14202); 82 (66-14132); and 83 (66-14131).

National Gallery of Canada:

Page 10.

National Library of Canada:

Pages 25 top (L 6857); 25 bottom (L 6853); 26 (L 6856); 32 (L 6849); 37 (L 6973); 38 left (L 6850); 39 bottom (L 6848); and 49 (L 6852).

Notman Photographic Archives, McCord Museum, McGill University:

Pages 15, 34, 35, 42 left and 43 top right.

Public Archives of Canada:

Pages 11 (C 40318); 13 (C 40313); 14 (C 1823); 16 (C 5955); 18 top (C 41157); 19 (C 2339); 20 and 21 (C 2393); 23 (C 13246); 24 (C 5954); 28 (C 2310); 29 (C 40334); 30 (C 63684); 31 (C 63896); 36 (C 22465); 38 right (C 4899); 39 top (C 42924); 40 top (PA 118011); 40 bottom (PA 30760); 41 left (C20869); 41 right

(PA 55080); 42 right (PA 8511); 43 top left (PA 30669); 43 bottom right (PA 30686); 44 bottom (C 4857); 45 (C 757); 50 (PA 60955); 51 (PA 61274); 52 (PA 61104); 53 (PA 69823); 54 right (C 18668); 55 left (PA 43518); 55 right (C 33922); 56 right (C 33927); 57 bottom (PA 48168); 58 (C 45356); 59 (PA 44970) and 84 bottom (PA 48188).

Ontario Hydro:

Pages 71 top and 73 right.

Oshawa Harbour Commission:

Page 79 top.

Queen's University Archives:

Page 43 bottom left.

Royal Ontario Museum: Sigmund Samuel Collection:

Pages 18 bottom, 20 and 33.

Saint Lawrence Seaway Development Corporation:

Pages 71 bottom left, 74 top left and 74 top right.

Toronto Harbour Commissioners:

Page 79 bottom.

Numbers in parenthesis are for identification. Illustrations on pages 25 top, 25 bottom, 26, 32, 37, 38, 39 bottom and 49 are from *Picturesque Canada* edited by G. M. Grant (2 vols; 880 pp.; 1882).

The following illustrations are from the Authority's photographic collection: pages 22, 68 right, 70 bottom left, 70 bottom right, 72 right, 76, 84 top, 85 top, 85 bottom right, 85 bottom left and 86 top. The collection also includes the following works by Hans van der Aa, St. Lambert, pages 62, 63, 64, 65, 66, 67 left: André Sima, Ottawa, page 68 left; and Bob Acciaro Photography, Lachine, page 87.

Pages 46, 71 bottom right and 74 bottom are from the author's own collection. He records his indebtedness to members of the staffs of all the organizations listed above for their assistance. Every effort has been made to identify and acknowledge accurately each of the illustrations. Advice of any inadvertent errors will be appreciated.

R.F.L.